Big Cats
For Kids

Amazing Animal Books
for Young Readers

by John Davidson

Mendon Cottage Books

JD-Biz Publishing

Read More Amazing Animal Books

Purchase at Amazon.com

Table of Contents

1. 10 Facts About Big Cats

If a naturalist uses the term of big cats, this usually will be talking about the four different kinds of cats that can roar, and these four different kinds of cats are very different in size from each other, and they also live in different places in the world. The first fact about all these big cats is that they are all carnivores, which means meat eaters, and this means that they do out hunting for their food a good deal of the time.

 The second fact about big cats is that they belong to a family group called the genus Panther and in the Panther group you will find lions, tigers, leopards, and jaguars. The third fact about big cats is that they unlike smaller cats do prefer to eat their food while they are laying down. The forth fact about big cats is that they mainly do their hunting at night, but there are some species of these big cats that do hunt only during the day. The fifth fact about big cats is they are very powerful climbers the big cats is no other than the leopard. The leopard is able to carry any prey up a tree, which is sometimes twice its own weight in description.

10 facts about big cats that are interesting and true do continue, and the number six fact is this tigers are considered to be the largest amid all big cats. Siberian tigers alone can achieve weights up to 700 pounds. The seventh fact about big cats is that Amur leopards are endangered from among the endangered list of world animals. The eighth fact about big cats is that only lions are the one big cat who lives in groups that are known as being prides. These prides have females that are all related to each other. The ninth fact about big cats is that mountain lions have longer back legs than legs in the front of their body, and this is something that works to their advantage, because it makes them truly strong jumpers because of their muscular back legs. The tenth and final fact about big cats is that tigers are hunted a great deal for not just their skin, but their very bones, and other assorted body parts that can be used as part of traditional Chinese medicine.

The ten facts listed here about big cats only show just how very unique and special big cats are. Therefore, we should truly appreciate them for being the wonderful animals that they, and which we have come to know and love as being part of the big animal kingdom.

2. Facts For Children About Leopards

Did you know that leopards are hunters that like to hunt at night and will often drag their food into a tree to keep it safe from other animals? Leopards are part of the cat family but unlike lions they like to be on their own.

You will be able to recognize a leopards by their spotted fur which is usually a cream and gold color, although a few leopards have a dark fur with black spots. Black leopards are often mixed up with panthers as people can't always tell them apart from a distance.

Leopards are solitary meaning they like their own company and often they will have a favorite area where they live, they usually try and avoid other leopards.

A leopard has a very powerful body and can run very fast sometimes up to 50 miles an hour. They can also swim and climb trees and jump over long distances.

An interesting thing to know is that a leopard's tail is nearly as long as its body, this helps it to balance and to turn fast when it needs to.

© kyslynskyy - Fotolia.com

Female leopards usually have two or three cubs at a time and the cubs stay with their mother until they are about 2 years old, then they go and live on their own.

Most leopards are found in parts of South Africa though you may find some in parts of India, China and Malaysia.

3. What Do You Think A Wildcat Is?

Have you ever heard of a Wildcat before? What do you think it is? What would it look like to you? I never really knew, until I spent some time at the zoo studying them.

Here is what I found out about them! First, they are not very big cats. They are nowhere near the size of lions or tigers.

© Nadine Haase - Fotolia.com

They are actually closer to the size of the kind of cat you might have in your house! Do you have cat? Or do you have a friend with one? A Wildcat is probably just a little bigger than those kinds of cats.

Wildcats usually have legs that are a little longer, and bodies that are a little bigger than the cat at your house? Why do they look so similar though?

Many people think that the kind of cat that you have at your house is related to the Wildcat. A very long time ago, many people would take Wildcats and put them in their homes, to get rid of mice or other rodents.

Many Wildcats have a lot of different colors in their fur, just like cats that you might have at your house. But most of them have a long black stripe down their back,

You should come to the zoo and see what Wildcats look like too.

4. Endangered Big Cats

Research figures show that the number of endangered animals especially cats is increasing dramatically. Meaning that generations to come will not be lucky enough to see most of the endangered cats in flesh since they are all dying at a rapid speed.

Some of the common reasons that contribute to the extinction of such animals include poaching, habitat destruction and thriving fur. All animals have a balanced ecosystem and niche environment that they co-exist. However, if the balance is not proportional then, the population will definitely expand or diminish.

Some of the most endangered cats in the world include the tiger and cheetah. Research has shown that the population of these cats is going down every single year. However, game reserves are trying their best to keep them alive.

Most of these animals can only be found in Africa and some parts of Asia. It is advisable that you make a point of visiting national parks and game reserves in order to see them while they are still alive.

5. Big Cats Habitat

© Joanne Stemberger - Fotolia.com

People are fascinated by tigers, lions and cheetah as they are becoming aware of their lives which they lead. They are also called the big cat. This awareness and curiosity lead to the need to protect them. Seeing them in their natural habitat is one of the most rewarding experiences. This experience can be enhanced by learning about the relationship of the big cat habitat with its surroundings.

These big cats are adapted to the forest environment. Large reserves are there for protecting these big cats habitats. Bostawa safari is the place of these cats' habitats. The cats of east Africa are also very famous worldwide. Lion, cheetah and tigers are considered as the three greatest cats of Africa as they are the legends which are passionate all over the world. The lion are called the king of beast as they are a cat of beauty and strength. Cheetah is the fastest animal on earth. Leopards are the most elusive of all the big cats.

6. All About Cougars

© hgrose - Fotolia.com

Cougars are also called Mountain Lions. They are also called pumas and panthers. They live in North and South America and can adapt to a lot of climates, however, most of the cougars in the mid-west and

---

eastern United States have been killed. So today, cougars mostly live in the Western part of the United States and Canada, in the Rocky Mountains, and also in many parts of South America.

The cougar will not roar like a lion does, but it is still and excellent hunter. The cougar likes to live in areas where there is a lot of thick brush and rocks because it uses these to hide from its prey when it is hunting.

The cougar is a meat eater, it does not eat plants. In North America, it often eats deer, but it will also eat smaller animals like squirrels or raccoons. It is also known to eat even larger animals, like cattle. Cougars hunt and live alone, they are a solitary animal.

Cougars are very fast and agile. They are the 4th largest of the large cats. Adult male cougars are about eight feet long on average, from the nose to the tail. The average male cougar weighs 140 pounds, but larger males can weigh as much as 220 pounds. The average female cougar weighs about 95 pounds.

7. Have You Ever Heard Of An Ocelt?

Have You Ever Heard Of An Ocelot?

Have you ever heard of a cat called an Ocelot? I had not. So I did some research, and then I went to the zoo, to see one for myself!

Ocelots are very warm animals. They love it where it warm, so some of them live very far south, like in Mexico. Most even live in South America!

They look very interesting! I noticed they are not large cats, like lions, tigers, or leopards. They are more like the size of the kind of cat you might have at home.

But They probably don't look like the cat you might have at home. The colors and patterns on their fur look almost exactly those on leopards or jaguars!

This is why some people call them dwarf, or small or little, leopards. They have many dark spots all over their tan fur.

They are also very skinny, or lithe, animals. They have long skinny legs, long skinny bodies, and long skinny tails. Everything about them seems to be long and skinny!

© hgrose - Fotolia.com

They are very pretty small cats. They walk around like very proud animals!

You should take an adult online with you, and look for pictures of an Ocelot. Then, go to the zoo, and see if you can find one in real life!

8. About African Cheetahs

About African Cheetahs

Cheetahs are a large cat the live in most of Africa and portions of the Middle East. Cheetahs are the fastest animal in the world. They can run as fast as 75 miles per hour for short distances. Cheetahs can also accelerate very quickly, they can go from zero to sixty miles per hour in less than five seconds.

Cheetahs have a deep chest and narrow waste. Their fur is tan and has round black spots on it. The underside of a cheetah has white fur. Full grown cheetahs weigh between fifty and one hundred pounds. It is difficult to tell the difference between male and female cheetahs by looking at them and the males and females are not much different in size and weight.

Cheetahs have retractable claws, giving them extra grip when they are running fast. Cheetahs also have large nostrils, and very large lungs, and heart, all of these things work together to allow the cheetah to run and accelerate very quickly. In addition to getting very good traction with its retractable claws, cheetahs use their tail to help them make very sharp terms, which the need to capture their prey while hunting.

© Anna Omelchenko - Fotolia.com

The cheetah is a species that is vulnerable to extinction, because it cannot adapt well to new environment and it is very difficult to breed them in zoos.

9. The African Caracal

The caracal is a member of the cat family. They live primarily in Africa and Asia. They have the honor of being the fastest small cat in all of Africa. Caracals usually weigh from 30 to 50 pounds, 3 feet long and about 1 and a half feet tall. The coloring of these beautiful cats is gray or a sandy red. The word caracal means black-eared in Turkish. They are called this because they have long ears with tufts of black hair are usually around 2 inches long.

© Duncan Noakes - Fotolia.com

They are carnivorous which means that they mainly eat meat. They hunt animals such as rodents, birds, and even small antelopes. They

---

have strong hindquarters which allows them to catch birds that fly low in the air.

The average life span for the caracal is 19 years in the wild. They generally spend the first year of their life with their mothers. Once the first year has passed, caracals tend to be solitary animals, though they sometimes hunt in pairs.

The caracal is a protected species in about half of the areas that it is found. They are hunted for their meat and fur. In certain countries, they are also a problem animal for farmers because they hunt livestock.

10. Big Cats Diet

Big cats require balanced diets just as human beings do. The following components should be included in the diet of the big cats.

© Eric Gevaert - Fotolia.com

Proteins and fats

They require a diet that is rich in protein and fat. The protein and fat concentration should even be higher than that of other carnivorous animals.

Vitamins

For them to be healthy they should be supplied with foods that are high in vitamins, especially vitamin C and D.

Amino acids

If we fail to give them food that have sufficient amounts of amino acids, they will lose their vision easily thus reducing their lifespan.

Calcium

Calcium in the diet of a big cat helps in preventing metabolic and reproductive ailments.

Generally, big cats should be given balanced diets. It is wrong to think that they depend on meat alone because every nutrient is equally important for the health of big cats. We should not fail to supply all the necessary nutrients.

11. Cubs Or Baby Big Cats

The following are facts you should know about cubs or baby big cats

1.Cubs of lions have a gestation period of 110 days, this means they are in their mothers tummy almost 4 months, before they are born.

© Alan Lucas - Fotolia.com

2. Cubs of a lion are born in a litter comprising a minimum of one baby up to six babies.

3. The mother lion goes for isolation for a period of about eight weeks in a safe place to give birth. This is because the cubs are defenseless during birth.

4. Cubs of lions face danger from predators such as leopards, hyenas, jackals, martial eagles and pythons in the jungle.

5. Female lions help each other in taking care of the cubs after the female lion returns to the pride after giving birth.

6. Lion cubs begin eating meat at the start of three months. They nurse for a period of about 6 months and will take advantage of any teat available even the one not belonging to their mother in case the female allows it.

7. Leopard cubs will always nurse strictly from their mother's teat.

8. Lion cubs begin hunting at the of one year, before that they depend on left over from the other lions kill.

12. Tigers

What Are Some Things That Makes Tigers Special?

Tigers are not only some of the most beautiful of all predators, but they are also some of the most feared by mankind, in addition. However these wonderful big cats are every inch special, and here are some reasons why they are so special. Not only is the tiger the biggest when it comes to being a cat species it is also the third largest meat eater on land, the two other biggest meat eaters are brown bears and polar bears.

Tigers are also known for their very known dark vertical stripes and these dark vertical stripes are set against fur which is reddish-orange in color and a bit lighter on the underside. There is also different species of tigers that range from the Bengal to the Siberian to the Malayan to the Indochinese to beyond.

What are some things that make tigers special? Well a few things have already been listed about the Tigers but there is a few more details that does separate them from other living animals. Tigers seem to have a tremendous longevity which means that they live very long both in zoos and out in the wild. The average tiger can live anywhere from twenty to twenty-six years and they are considered to be solitary, territorial, and also very social animals. All these things combined together are what makes tigers both very fascinating and very one of a kind creatures in their own ways.

13. A Cat Called a Serval

One of my very favorite cats has a very strange name. It is called a Serval. Have you ever heard of this kind of cat?

It is a very pretty cat. Let me tell you some about how it looks.

First, it is a very skinny cat. It is not fat at all! It has a long skinny tail, long legs that make it look tall, and a long skinny body.

But it is not a small cat either! Some can weigh as much as 40 pounds! Some of them can also be as long as long as 36 inches, and that does not include their tail.

They do have very pretty fur though. And a lot of variety as well! Some are very pretty tan colors, with many dark spots all over.

Some of them are bright white, with dark spots that look almost gray. These ones look like they belong in the winter time.

And some are all black! But these ones are very rare.

© Sarah Cheriton-Jones - Fotolia.com

Servals like it to be very hot. They like warm weather the best. In fact, in the wild, all servals are native to Africa!

Next time you are at the zoo, keep your eye out for my favorite cat.

14. Snow Leopards: King of The Frozen Mountains

© veneratio - Fotolia.com

The snow leopard is a rare cat from the mountains of Central Asia. One of the smaller of the "big cats," the snow leopard can weigh between 60 and 100 pounds. Their short, bulky build and thick fur is perfect for keeping warm in their cold mountain habitat. They also have a long tail to help them balance as they hop from rock to rock. Their dusky yellowish grey fur helps them blend into the rocks around them, so that the prey they hunt never see them coming.

Favorite foods of the snow leopard include mountain sheep called Bharal, rabbits, and birds. Because food can sometimes be scarce, they will eat almost anything, and unlike most other cats are even able to eat plants such as grass and twigs.

Snow leopards live on their own, only coming together when it is time to breed. Mother leopards will raise their babies on their own inside a den. The dens are usually in a protected outcropping of rock where the babies will be safe.

The snow leopard is an endangered cat, due in large part to habitat loss and being hunted for their thick fur. Some estimates say that there are only around 5,000 snow leopards left in the wild.

15. The Bobcat, North America's Wildcat

Bobcats are the most common wildcat in all of North America. They live near the Canadian border and throughout the US and Mexico. They are nocturnal animals so they are not normally visible to humans. Bobcats are about double the size of your average house cat. Their short "bobbed" tails are the reason for their name. They are usually brown to gray in coloring with black markings on their fur.

© JackF - Fotolia.com

They are solitary animals and leave their mother when they are just 10-12 months old. Their average life span is just around 13 years. Rabbits, squirells, and rodents are the most common animals that they hunt for food. Usually, they live in a main den and have multiple other dens that they use for shelter. They need these other dens because their territory can range up to 20 square miles.

The growls from a bobcat are known to be quite deep and scary. Most people are shocked to realize that the growl comes from the bobcat because it seems like it should come from a much bigger animal. The bobcat only grows to be about 23 inches tall and 41 inches long. The males can weigh up to 28 pounds and the females to 18 pounds.

16. Why I Love The Jaguarundi

Do you want to know what my favorite cat is? I really like a cat called the Jaguarundi. It is probably my favorite cat!

I don't mean I want to take one home, they are not the kind of cat you can have in your house. They are wild cats. But I still love them. Why?

Well first, I like them because they are very pretty cats. They do not have big, tall ears. They have very short ears. Their ears are very round, too. They are not pointy ear like some cats have.

I also like them because they have such short legs. Their legs look like are very small compared to their bodies, which makes them cute to me. But their legs are still very powerful. They can jump very far with them.

Also, they do not have stripes or spots! Some cats like tigers or jaguars have stripes and spots all over them. Those can be a little scary to look at. The Jaguarundi has all one color though.

Sometimes, they have little dark markings around their face, which looks a little bit like they have make up on.

Can you see why I love this small cat? You should see if you can find one the next time you visit the zoo.

17. The Lynx - A Majestic Cat

The Lynx cat is truly very majestic. What does it look like? I never really new, until I saw some up close. Here is what I noticed!

© byrdyak - Fotolia.com

First, I saw that a Lynx has beautiful long ears, that have hair on the end that stick straight up. That makes the ears look even taller than they actually are.

The Lynx also have great big paws, with a lot of fur on them. They have very soft, very warm fur on the bottom of their paws, and in between their toes. This is to protect their paws from the cold snow, just like your boots!

The next thing I noticed about a Lynx is how their eyes almost glow in the dark! Did you know that is where their name actually comes from? In a very old language, there was a word that meant "brightness" that sounded a little like the worn "Lynx."

The last thing I noticed about them was their color! Some parts of them, especially their belly was fluffy white, almost like snow. Other parts were tan or brown with little black spots!

After seeing them at the zoo, I can tell you now, I love the Lynx! They are very pretty big cats!

18. What Are Pumas?

Pumas are very large powerful wild cats. They look very similar to leopards except that they don't have marks on their body, which is usually a light brownish color. Pumas have bright green eyes, and if you look carefully you will see that their front legs are shorter than their back legs, and that they have very long tails, and small heads with strong jaws.

Pumas can be known by different names and are often called cougars or panthers or even mountain lions. But they don't like to mix with other animals and prefer to be on their own.

Pumas can be found in Africa and Asia and also in America. They prefer to live in areas that have forests, and swamps and grassy plains. They eat large mammals like deer, but will also eat birds and rabbits and other smaller animals.

A baby puma is called a cub and when the female has a litter she will usually produce between one and four cubs.

Male pumas can grow to 8 feet in height and can weigh up to 250 pounds. They have very good hearing and eyesight and sharp claws which helps them when hunting food or protecting themselves from attacks. A puma can jump up to 20 feet which makes them hard to catch.

© Fotomicar - Fotolia.com

19. What Is A Jaguar?

A jaguar is the third biggest cat in the world and can be found mainly in South America in and around the Amazon River basin.

A jaguar can be up to six feet long, from the end of their nose to the end of their tail, and are sometimes grow to three feet in height. When it is born a jaguar weighs about two pounds, but as it gets older it usually reaches a weight of about 120 pounds although there have been a few jaguars that have weighed nearly 300 pounds.

© S.R.Miller - Fotolia.com

Jaguars are easily recognized by their unusual spotted coats, although the spots are more like splotches that spots. Having these splotches on their skin makes it easy for the Jaguar to hide in the trees and bushes, so they can hide from other dangerous animals or hunters.

Jaguars like to spend their time on the ground and you will usually find them in rainforests, and out in the grasslands. They have big padded paws that let them move silently through the forest, and sometimes they will climb into trees to rest or hunt.

Jaguars like to hunt at night and have very good eyesight and sharp teeth and are known to like eat over 80 different kinds of small animals. Sometimes they will even go into the water to snatch at fish or turtles.

20. What Are Lions?

Did you know that lions are the second largest cat in the world after tigers? A male lion can weigh as much as 400 pounds and a female usually weighs about 290 pounds. The heaviest lion ever discovered weighed 826 pounds.

Lions can run very fast at nearly 50 miles an hour but they can't do that for very long as they get tired. When they are angry or want to attract attention they can roar really loudly and can be heard several miles away.

Most lions live in Africa and often live in groups which are called prides. Prides usually consist of male lions, female lionesses and young lion cubs.

It's easy to recognize a male lion as they have a very noticeable mane surrounding their head, these are supposed to attract female lions to them.

Some countries have adopted the lion as their national animal and you will often see a lion shown on their flags. England and Singapore are two countries that have adopted the lion as their national animal.

© Lsantilli - Fotolia.com

Lions usually live for about 12 years in the wild if they are not injured or attacked. The male lion is a better hunter than the female lioness and will usually do all the hunting for food for the lionesses and cubs in the pride.

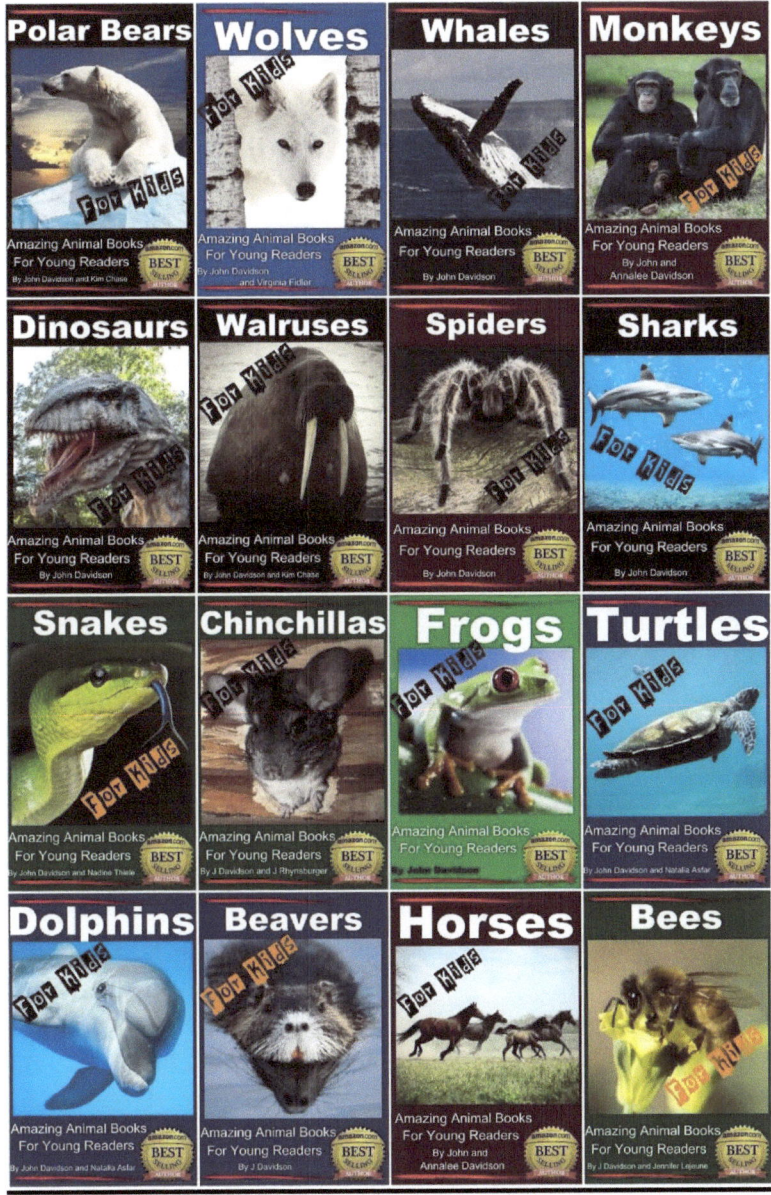

Horses
For Kids

Amazing Animal Books
For Young Readers
By John and
Annalee Davidson

Ponies
For Kids

AmazingAnimalBooks

Rachel Smith

Ten Amazing
Horses
For Kids

Nature Books for Kids
JD-Biz Publishing
K. Bennett

Akhal-Teke
"The Golden Horse
of the desert"
For Kids

Nature Books for Kids
JD-Biz Publishing
K. Bennett

Suffolk Punch
"The Gentle Giant"
For Kids

Nature Books for Kids
JD-Biz Publishing
K. Bennett

Shires
"The great Horse"
For Kids

Nature Books for Kids
JD-Biz Publishing
K. Bennett

Colonial Spanish
"Horse of the Americas"
For Kids

Nature Books for Kids
JD-Biz Publishing
K. Bennett

Canadian
"The Little Iron Horse"
For Kids

Nature Books for Kids
JD-Biz Publishing
K. Bennett

Cleveland Bays
"History and Future"
Horses For Kids

Nature Books for Kids
JD-Biz Publishing
K. Bennett

Top Ten Dog Breeds For Kids
Amazing Animal Books For Young Readers
Kisha Bennett & John Davidson

German Shepherds
Dog Books for Kids
K. Bennett

Bulldogs
Dog Books for Kids
K. Bennett

Dachshund
Dog Books for Kids
K. Bennett

Poodles
Dog Books for Kids
K. Bennett

Labrador Retrievers
Dog Books for Kids
K. Bennett

Rottweilers
Dog Books for Kids
K. Bennett

Boxers
Dog Books for Kids
K. Bennett

Golden Retrievers
Dog Books for Kids
K. Bennett

Puppies
Dog Books For Kids
Amazing Animal Books
By John Davidson

Beagles
Dog Books for Kids
K. Bennett

Yorkshire Terriers
Dog Books for Kids
K. Bennett

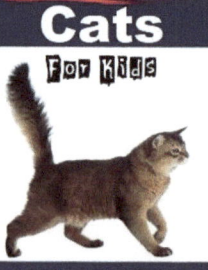

Dogs Top Ten Dog Breeds For Kids
Amazing Animal Books For Young Readers
Zahra Jazeel & John Davidson

Cats For Kids
Amazing Animal Books For Young Readers
K. Bennett & John Davidson

Foxes For Kids
Amazing Animal Books For Young Readers
Zahra Jazeel & John Davidson

Wolves For Kids
Amazing Animal Books For Young Readers
By John Davidson and Virginia Fidler

Publisher

JD-Biz Corp

P O Box 374

Mendon, Utah 84325

http://www.jd-biz.com/